# *Folded Paper*
# GIFT BOXES

Maria O.

## STACKPOLE
## BOOKS

# Contents

**Kokeshi**
pages 6, 33–35

**Pillow**
pages 14, 49

**Chrysanthemum**
pages 16, 51–53

**Hanging Box**
pages 18, 55–57

Copyright © 2013 by Stackpole Books
French edition copyright © 2011 by Dessain et Tolra/Larousse

Published by
STACKPOLE BOOKS
5067 Ritter Road
Mechanicsburg, PA 17055
www.stackpolebooks.com

Larousse
Editor: Colette Hanicotte
Editorial and art coordination: Corinne de Montalembert
Photography: Fabrice Besse, Cactus studio
Style: Sonia Roy, Cactus studio
Design and pagination: Susan Pak Poy
Cover design: Susan Pak Poy

Stackpole Books
Translation: Kathryn Fulton
Pagination: Tessa J. Sweigert
Cover design: Tessa J. Sweigert

Printed in U.S.A.
10 9 8 7 6 5 4 3 2 1
First edition
ISBN 978-0-8117-1143-2

Cataloging-in-Publication Data is on file with the Library of Congress

**Heart**
pages 8, 37–39

**Pocket**
pages 10, 41–43

**Handbag**
pages 12, 45–47

**Tepee**
pages 20, 59

**Pinwheel**
pages 22, 61–63

**Star**
pages 24, 65–67

**Flower**
pages 26, 69–71

**Diamond**
pages 28, 73

**Surprise**
pages 30–32, 75–79

# **Tips** for assembling the boxes

It's a true pleasure to make a little gift for someone, and if you can match the gift box to its contents, everything is perfect! This book is a collection of 13 original decorated boxes, with different patterns and colors, of course (24 boxes ready to fold, in all!). You will also find the template for each of these 13 designs, which will allow you to decorate them with the pattern of your choice, make them from your favorite paper, or leave them blank to decorate!

## Materials
You will need only a few things to make these boxes:
- a cutting board
- a ruler
- a utility knife
- scissors
- an embossing stylus or bone folder
- a glue stick

## How to assemble the boxes
Pick one of the boxes to make and tear out the perforated page, or trace the template onto:
- a solid-color sheet of paper, decorated on the back
- the back of a sheet of decorative paper

In either case, choose a somewhat heavy weight: 80 to 120 pounds.
You can also cut out a template to use as a pattern so you can make as many boxes as you want.

## Cutting
Cut along all the solid lines, using the ruler and utility knife, or the scissors if they seem easier to use to you.

## Scoring
Scoring helps ensure crisp folds. To do this, use a ruler to guide your embossing stylus or bone folder (you can also score the paper with a utility knife—with a great deal of care, as you have to be careful not to cut all the way through; just barely scratch the paper).
If you're making a box from one of the detachable pages, it's best to refer to the pattern to get the folds in just the right place.

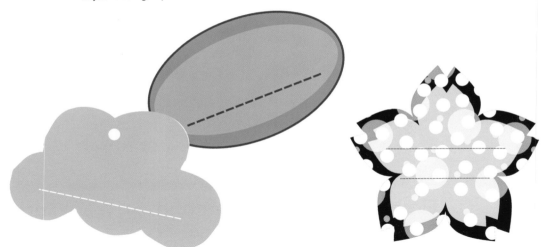

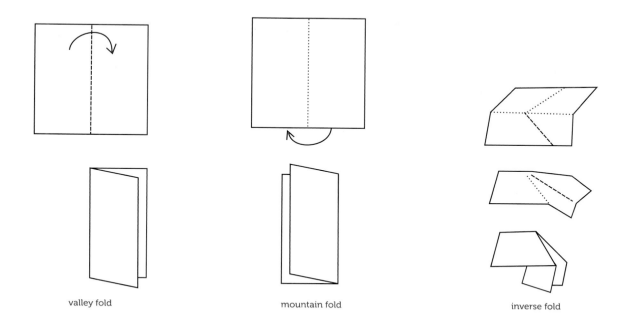

| valley fold | mountain fold | inverse fold |

## Folding

The folds called for in this book are almost all based on two kinds of folds: the valley fold and the mountain fold.

Valley folds are represented by dashed lines.

Mountain folds are represented by dotted lines.

A third fold type, inverse folds, are used only in the flower box.

**Note:** if you copy the pattern onto the inside of a box, all the folds should be reversed: the dotted lines become valley folds and the dashed lines become mountain folds.

## Gluing

An ordinary glue stick is all you need to put the boxes together. Put glue on the outsides of the tabs, which will be glued to the inside of the box. The only exception is the pinwheel box, which has tabs that are glued to the outside of the box (so you should put glue on the inner sides of these tabs).

## Tags

Choosing a tag can be a very simple way of personalizing a box, or of adapting it to the situation (a star or a Christmas tree for a Christmas gift, a bassinette for a new baby, a candle for a birthday). We've given you several tags for each box on the detachable pages so you can choose the one you like best. These tags are also interchangeable between the boxes.

The hardest part will be choosing which box to start with. Enjoy!

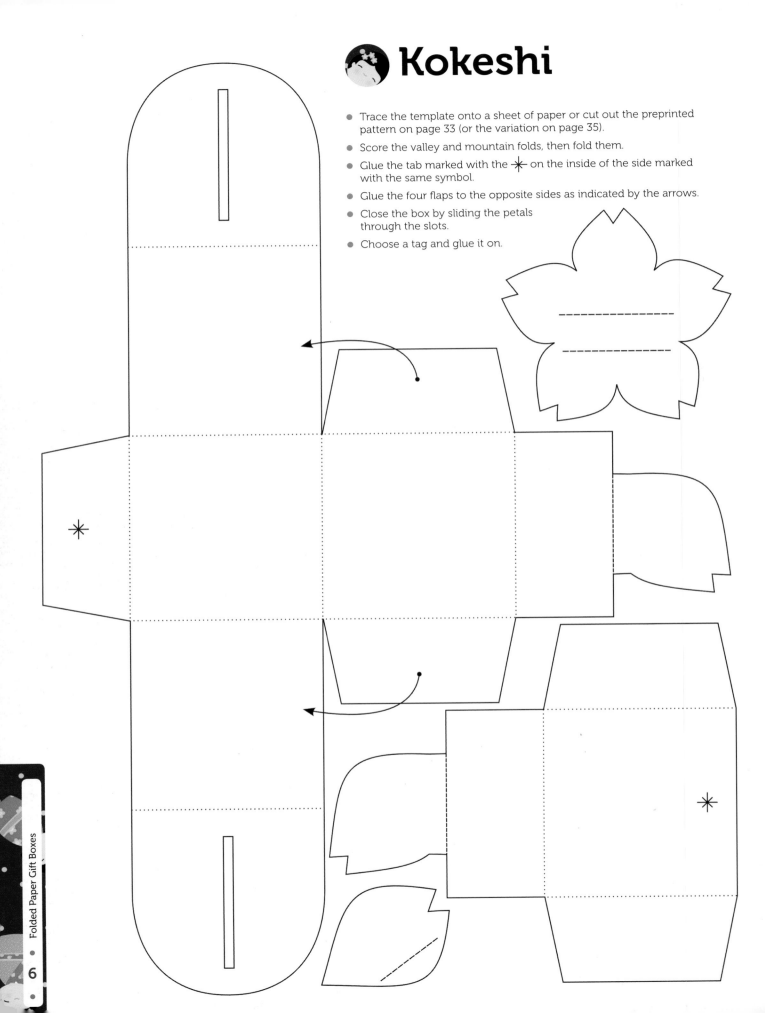

# Kokeshi

- Trace the template onto a sheet of paper or cut out the preprinted pattern on page 33 (or the variation on page 35).
- Score the valley and mountain folds, then fold them.
- Glue the tab marked with the ✳ on the inside of the side marked with the same symbol.
- Glue the four flaps to the opposite sides as indicated by the arrows.
- Close the box by sliding the petals through the slots.
- Choose a tag and glue it on.

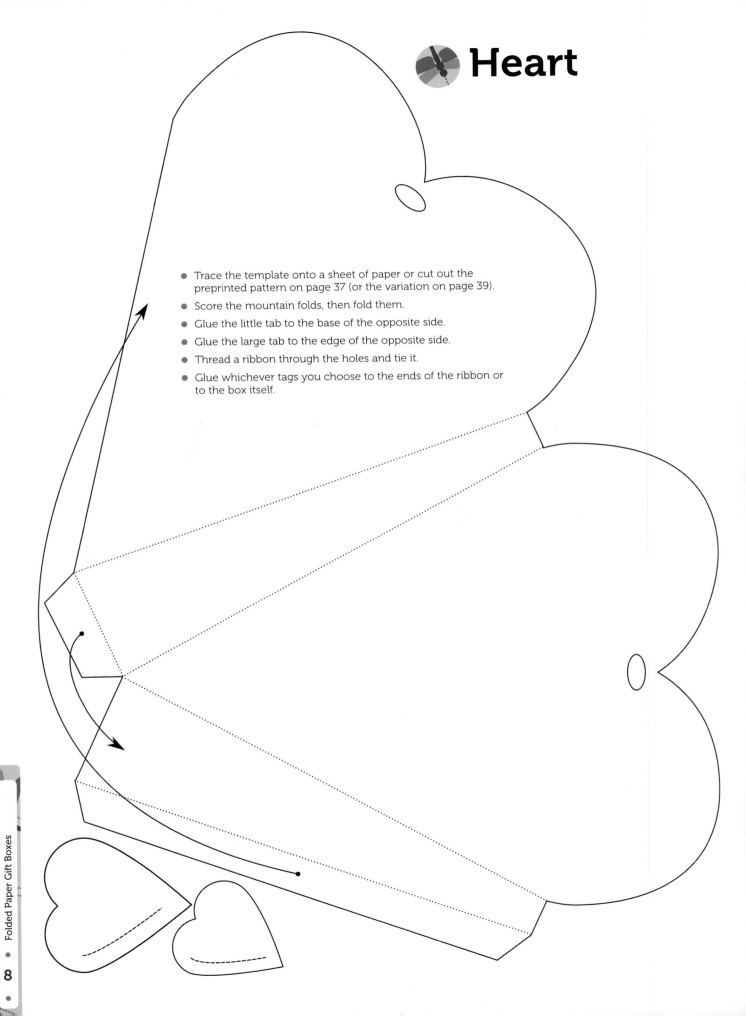

# Heart

- Trace the template onto a sheet of paper or cut out the preprinted pattern on page 37 (or the variation on page 39).
- Score the mountain folds, then fold them.
- Glue the little tab to the base of the opposite side.
- Glue the large tab to the edge of the opposite side.
- Thread a ribbon through the holes and tie it.
- Glue whichever tags you choose to the ends of the ribbon or to the box itself.

# Pocket

- Trace the template onto a sheet of paper or cut out the preprinted pattern on page 41 (or the variation on page 43).
- Score the valley and mountain folds, then fold them.
- Glue the side tab to the inside of the opposite side.
- Glue the three base tabs on the inside.
- After placing the gift in the box, close the flap with a dot of glue, then glue on the tag.

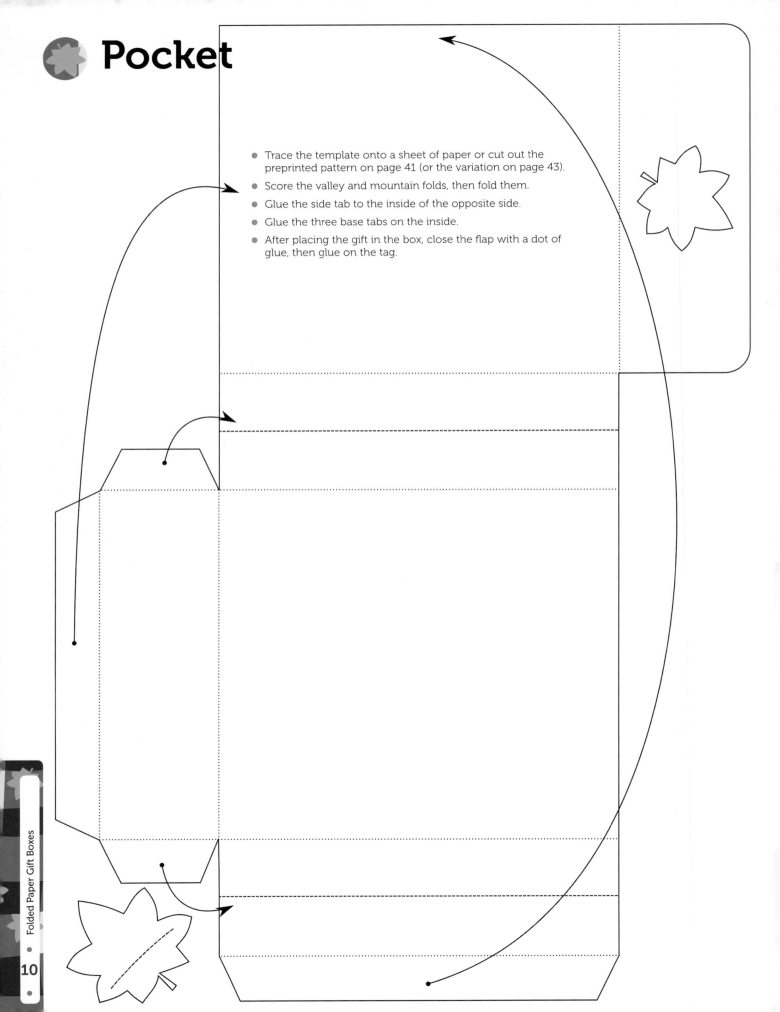

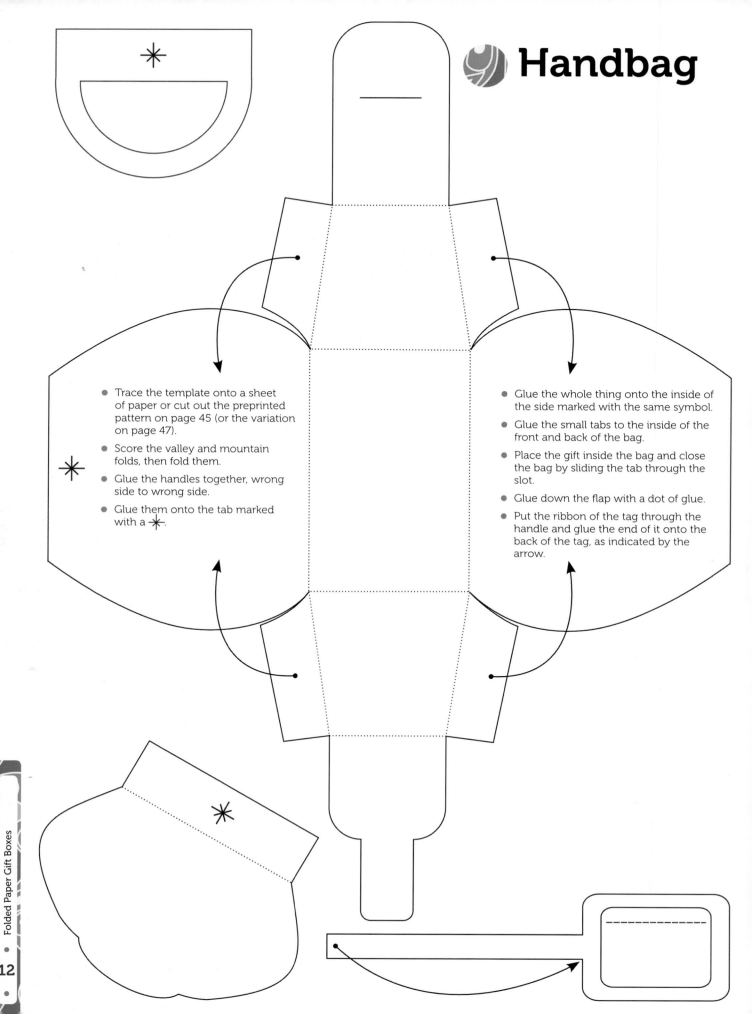

# Handbag

- Trace the template onto a sheet of paper or cut out the preprinted pattern on page 45 (or the variation on page 47).
- Score the valley and mountain folds, then fold them.
- Glue the handles together, wrong side to wrong side.
- Glue them onto the tab marked with a ✳.

- Glue the whole thing onto the inside of the side marked with the same symbol.
- Glue the small tabs to the inside of the front and back of the bag.
- Place the gift inside the bag and close the bag by sliding the tab through the slot.
- Glue down the flap with a dot of glue.
- Put the ribbon of the tag through the handle and glue the end of it onto the back of the tag, as indicated by the arrow.

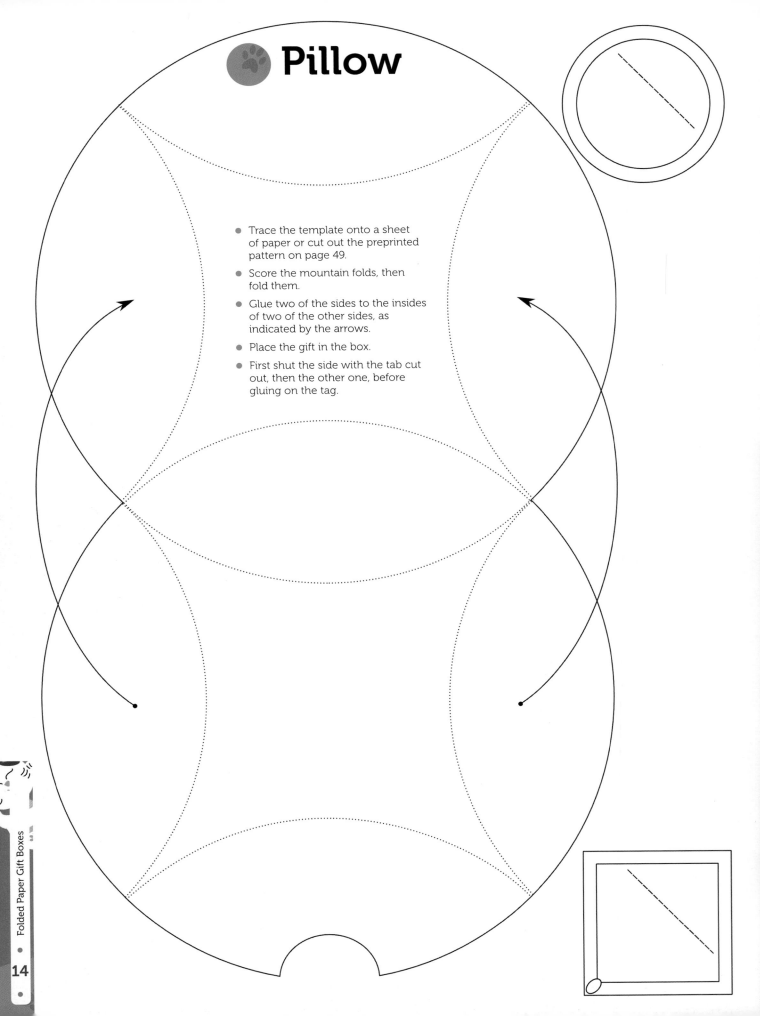

# Pillow

- Trace the template onto a sheet of paper or cut out the preprinted pattern on page 49.
- Score the mountain folds, then fold them.
- Glue two of the sides to the insides of two of the other sides, as indicated by the arrows.
- Place the gift in the box.
- First shut the side with the tab cut out, then the other one, before gluing on the tag.

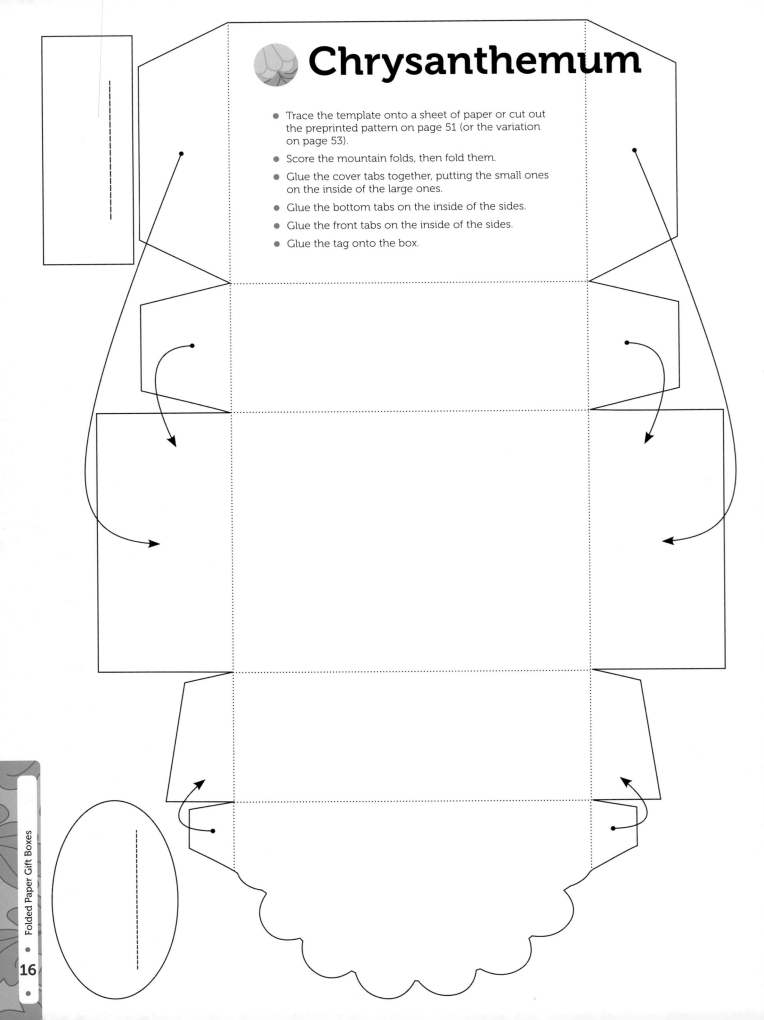

# Chrysanthemum

- Trace the template onto a sheet of paper or cut out the preprinted pattern on page 51 (or the variation on page 53).
- Score the mountain folds, then fold them.
- Glue the cover tabs together, putting the small ones on the inside of the large ones.
- Glue the bottom tabs on the inside of the sides.
- Glue the front tabs on the inside of the sides.
- Glue the tag onto the box.

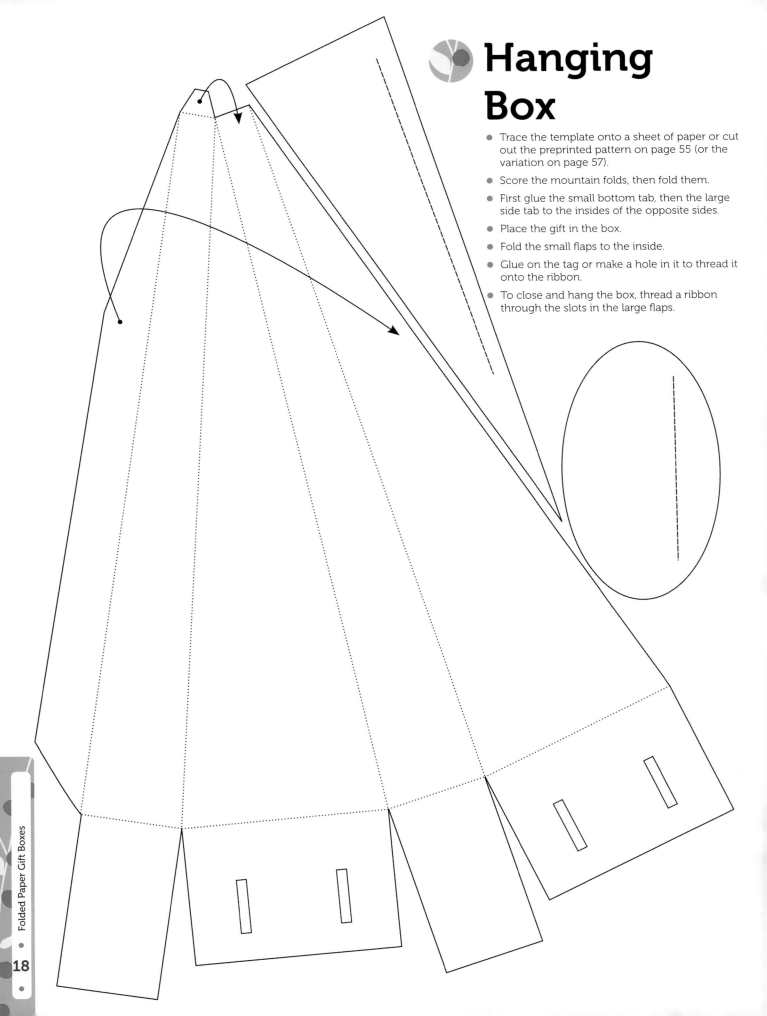

# Hanging Box

- Trace the template onto a sheet of paper or cut out the preprinted pattern on page 55 (or the variation on page 57).

- Score the mountain folds, then fold them.

- First glue the small bottom tab, then the large side tab to the insides of the opposite sides.

- Place the gift in the box.

- Fold the small flaps to the inside.

- Glue on the tag or make a hole in it to thread it onto the ribbon.

- To close and hang the box, thread a ribbon through the slots in the large flaps.

# Tepee

- Trace the template onto a sheet of paper or cut out the preprinted pattern on page 59.
- Score the mountain folds, then fold them.
- Cut the slots on the top flaps.
- Place the gift in the middle of the central square.
- Fold the large triangle flaps toward the center.
- Close the box by fitting the two split tabs into each other.

# Pinwheel

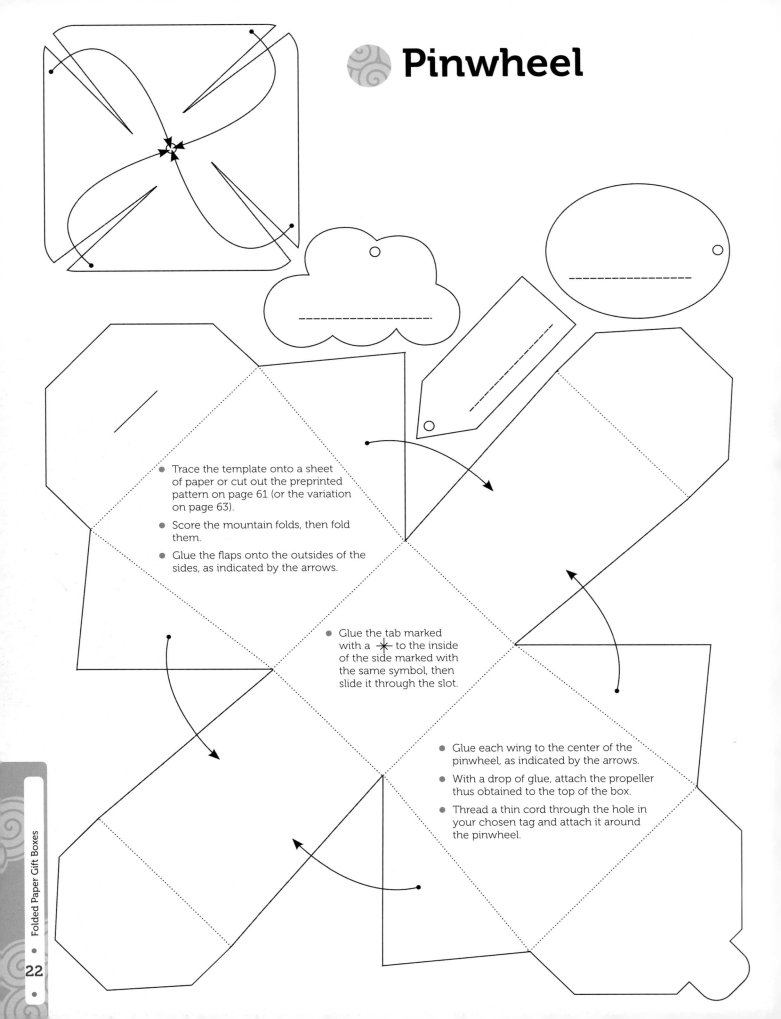

- Trace the template onto a sheet of paper or cut out the preprinted pattern on page 61 (or the variation on page 63).
- Score the mountain folds, then fold them.
- Glue the flaps onto the outsides of the sides, as indicated by the arrows.

- Glue the tab marked with a ✳ to the inside of the side marked with the same symbol, then slide it through the slot.

- Glue each wing to the center of the pinwheel, as indicated by the arrows.
- With a drop of glue, attach the propeller thus obtained to the top of the box.
- Thread a thin cord through the hole in your chosen tag and attach it around the pinwheel.

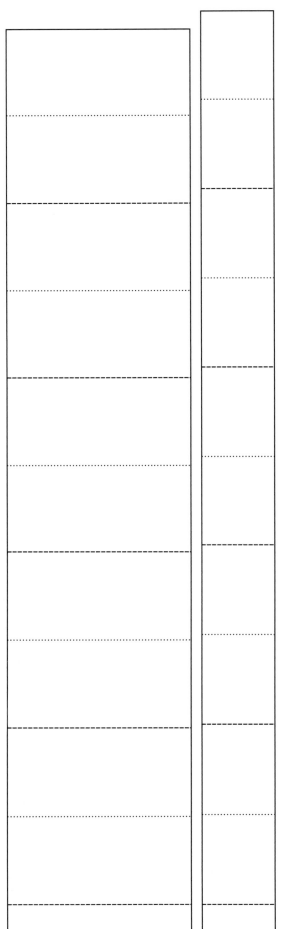

 **Star**

- Trace the template onto a sheet of paper or cut out the preprinted pattern on page 65 (or the variation on page 67).
- Score the mountain and valley folds, then fold them.
- Glue each tab of one of the stars to the lower edge of the large rectangle.
- Glue each tab of the remaining star to the lower edge of the other rectangle.
- Glue on the tag.

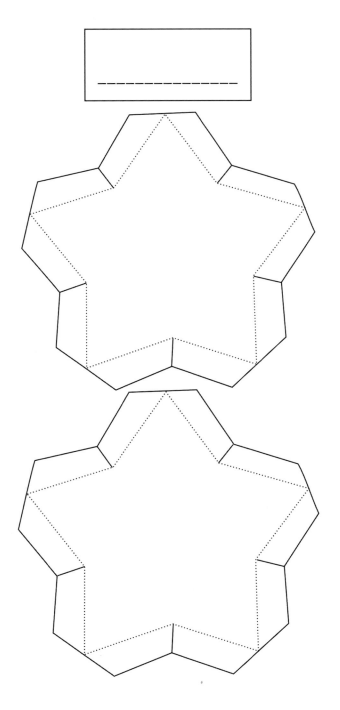

# Flower

- Trace the template onto a sheet of paper or cut out the preprinted pattern on page 69 (or the variation on page 71).
- Score the valley and mountain folds, then fold them.
- Glue the side tabs to the opposite sides.
- Glue the small tabs to the bottom.
- Place the gift in the box, then close it by folding the petals into the inside with inverse folds.
- Glue on the tag.

 # Diamond

- Trace the template onto a sheet of paper or cut out the preprinted pattern on page 73.
- Score the mountain and valley folds, then fold them.
- Place the gift in the central hexagon.
- Fold the sides back in to the center.
- Thread a ribbon through the slots and attach the tag to it.

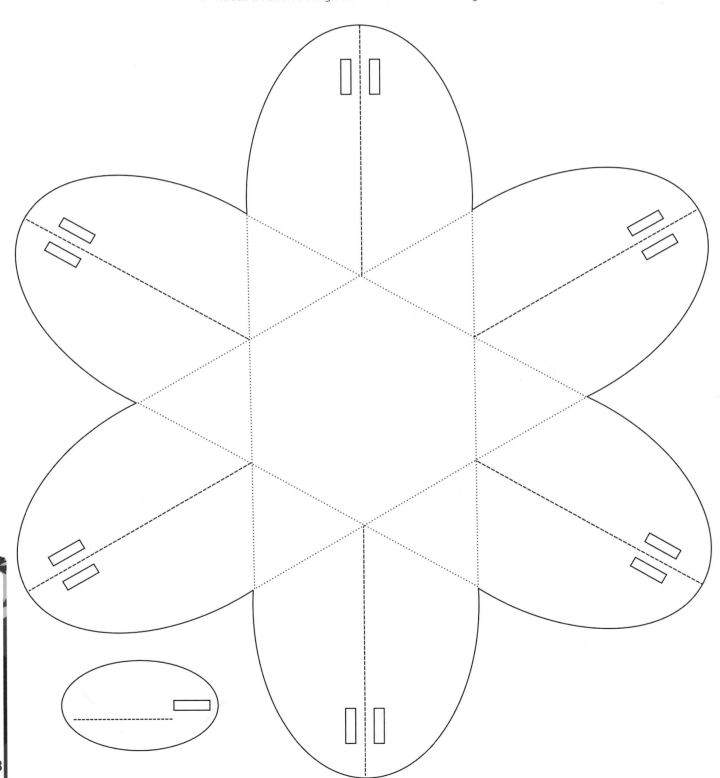

# Surprise

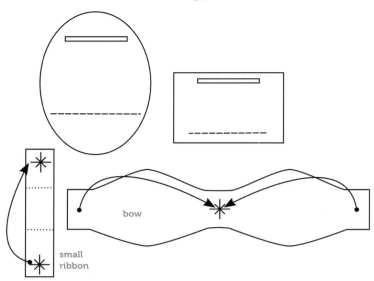

- Trace the template for the top and bottom (from page 32) onto a sheet of paper or cut out the preprinted patterns on page 75, 77, and 79.
- Score the mountain and valley folds, then fold them.

### To make the knot
- Glue the two ends of the knot into the center, as indicated by the arrows.
- Place the knot on the large ribbon so that the two stars are lined up.
- Finish the assembly by wrapping the small ribbon around the box and gluing the ends together on the back of the large ribbon.
- Slide the large ribbon through the slot in the tag.

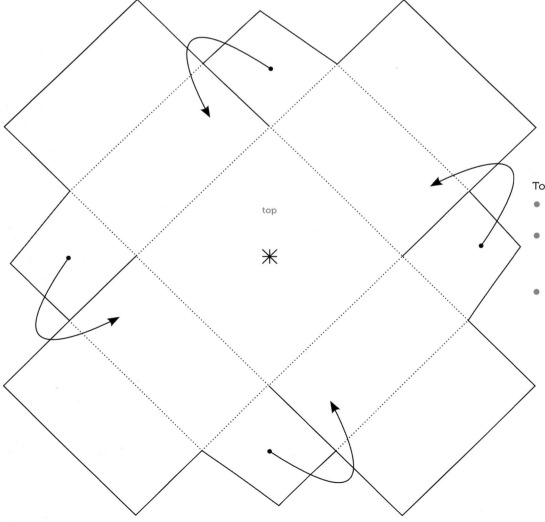

### To make the top
- Glue the small tabs to the insides of the sides.
- Place the bow on the top, gluing the ends of the large ribbon onto the insides of the large tabs.
- Fold the large tabs back into the inside of the top.

# Surprise

**To finish the box**

- Fold the sides of the bottom inward.
- Place the gift in the center.
- Close the box with the top.

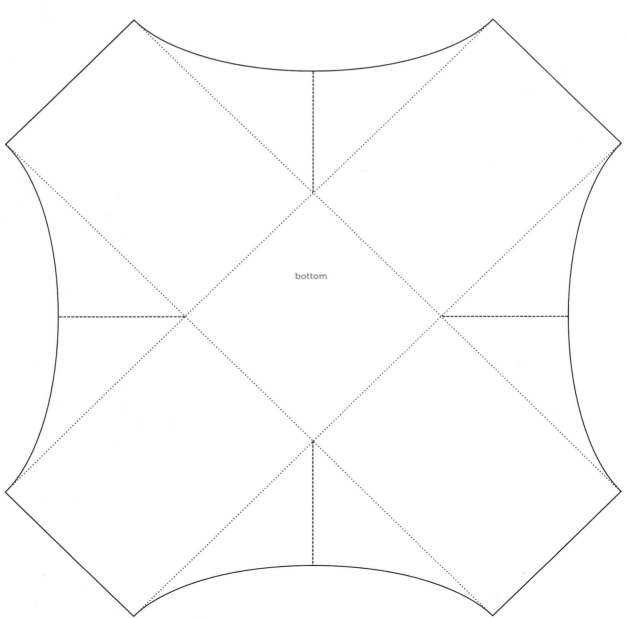

bottom

# Kokeshi
instructions on page 6

**Kokeshi**
instructions on page 6

**Pocket**
instructions on page 10

**Pocket**
instructions on page 10

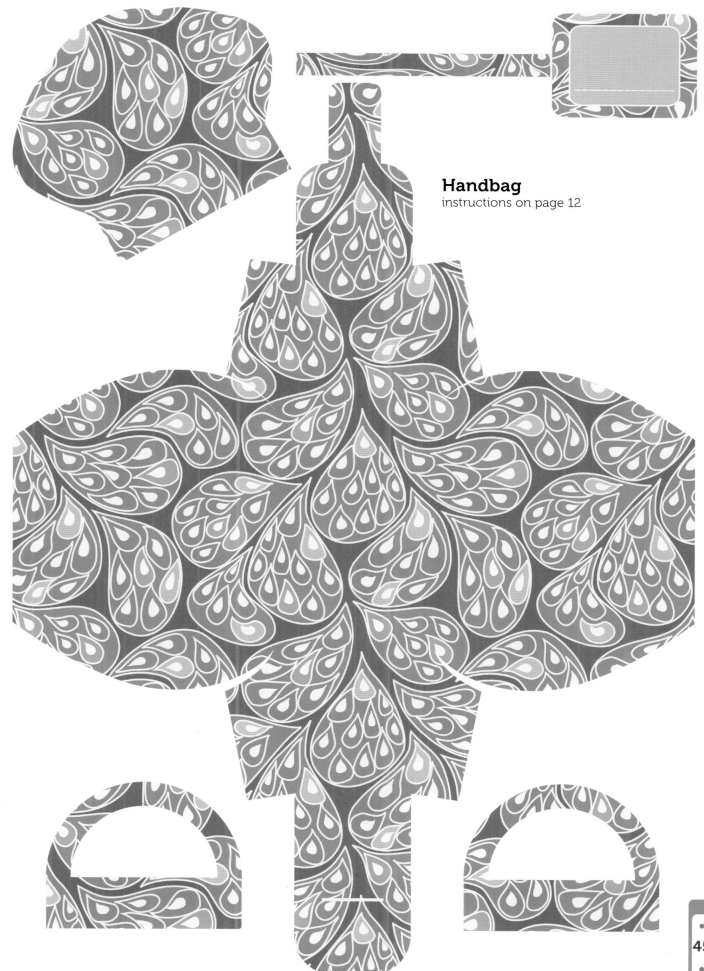

**Handbag**
instructions on page 12

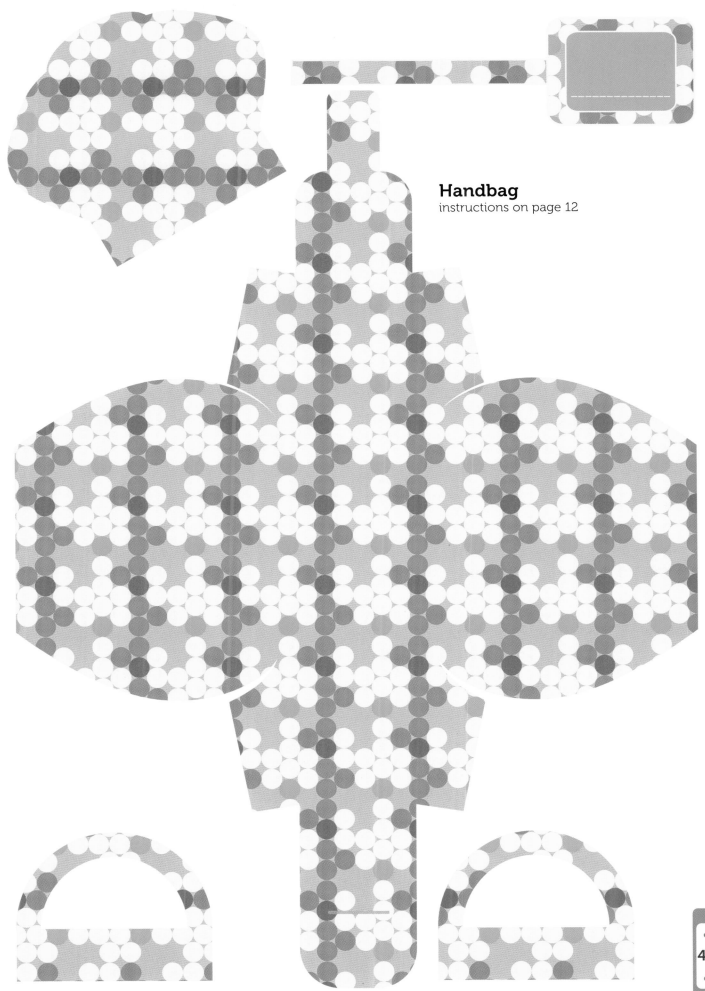

**Handbag**
instructions on page 12

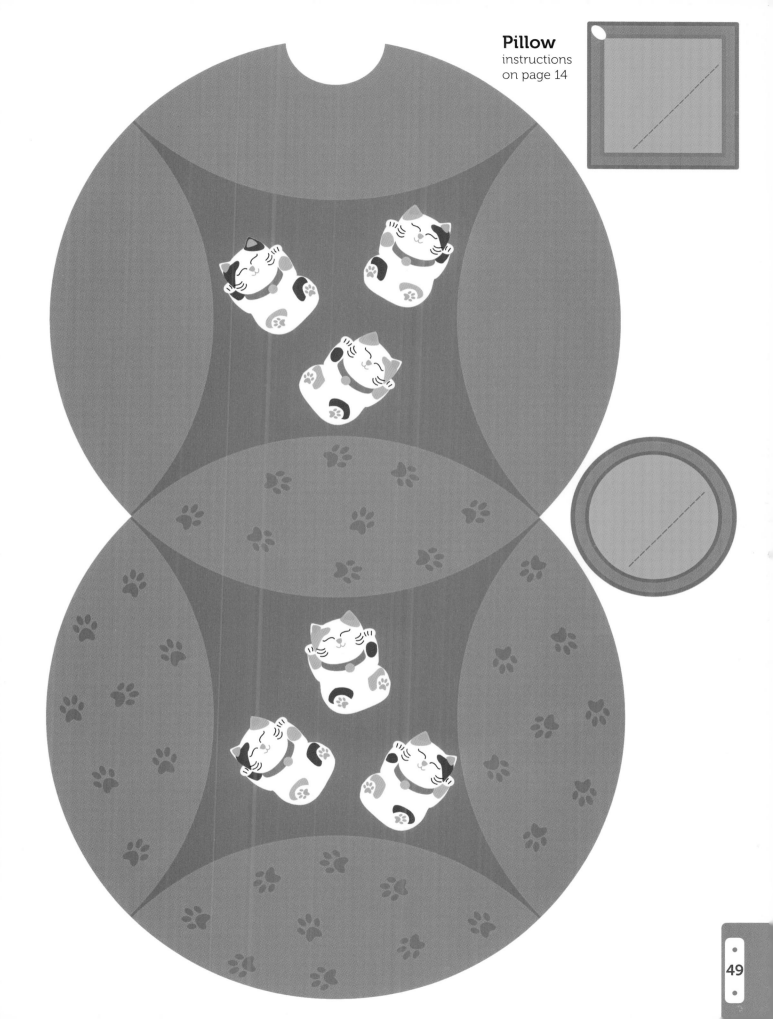

**Pillow**
instructions
on page 14

49

# Chrysanthemum

instructions on page 16

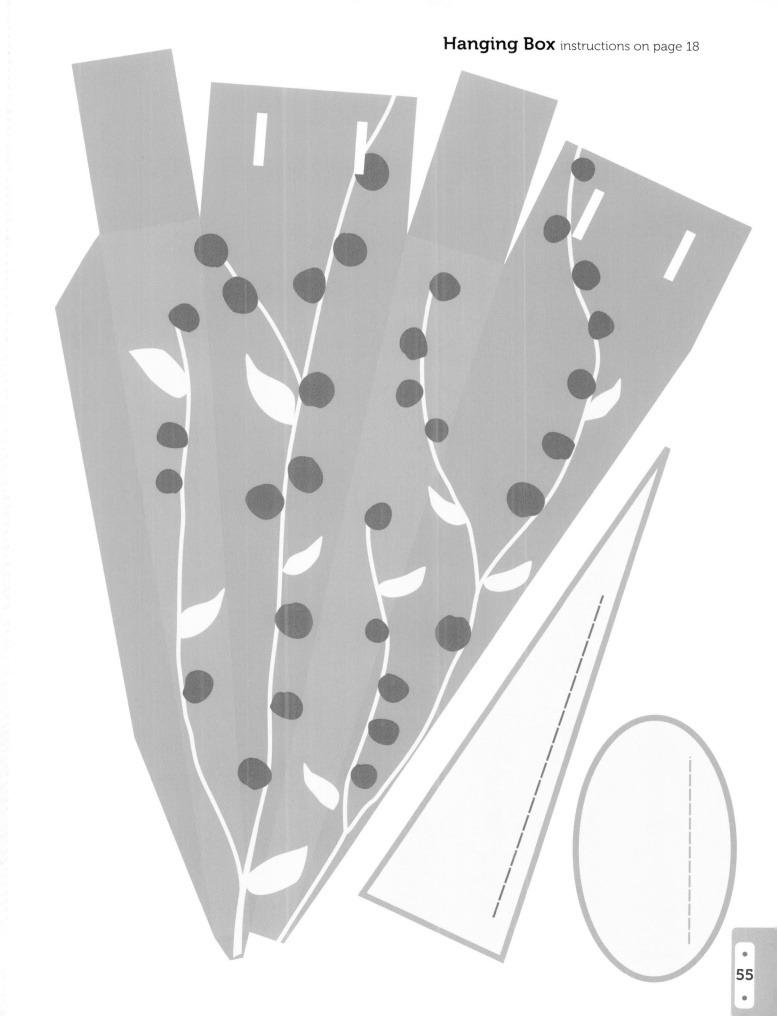

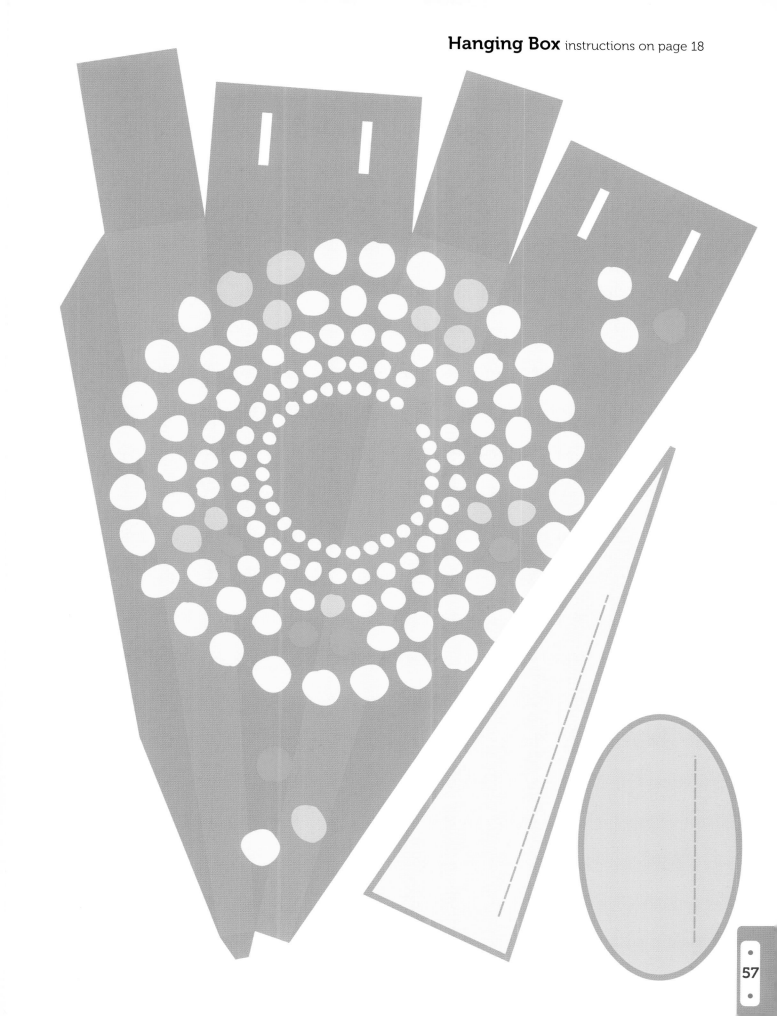

Pinwheel instructions on page 22

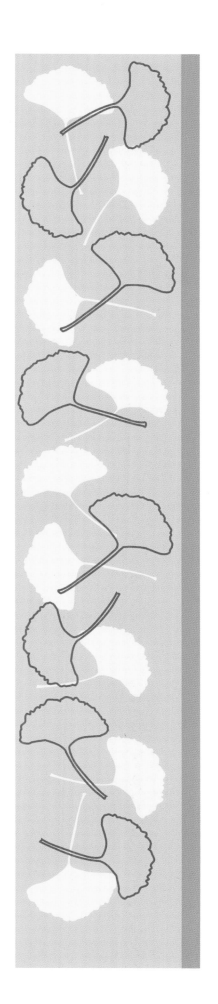

**Star**
instructions on page 24

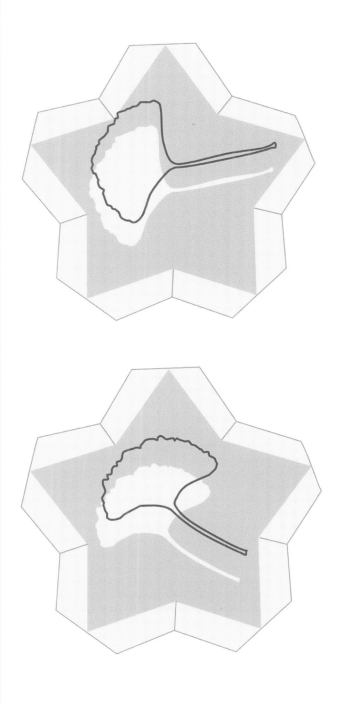

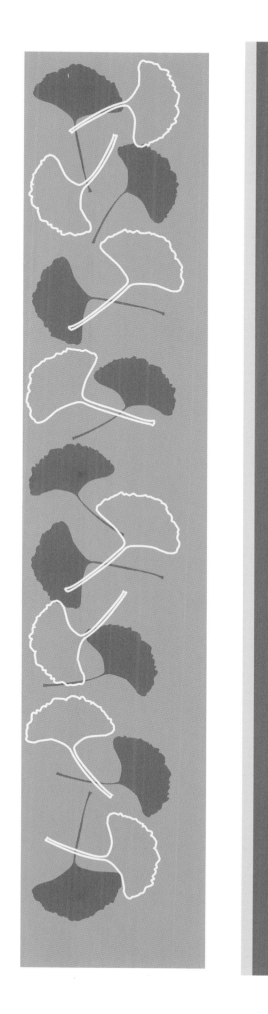

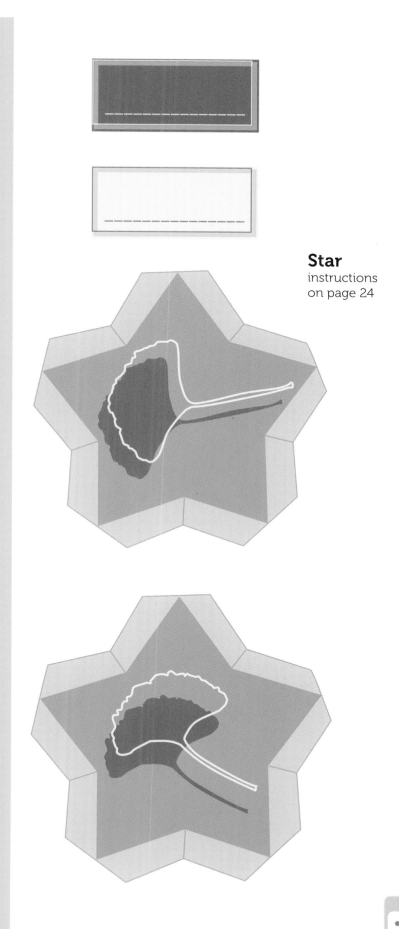

**Star**
instructions
on page 24

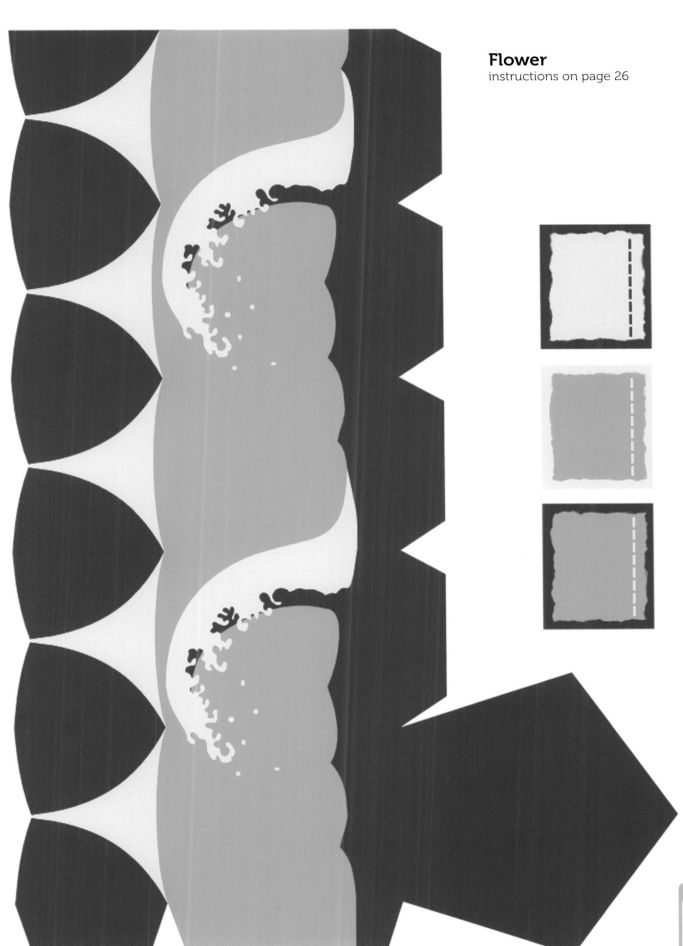

**Flower**
instructions on page 26

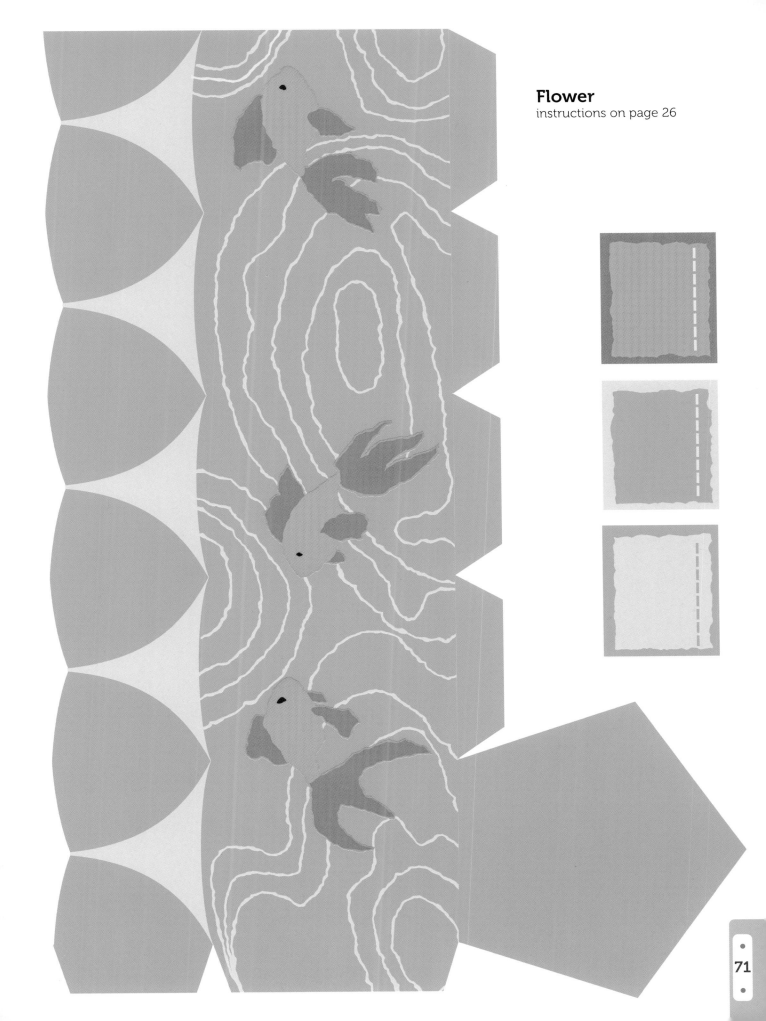

# Flower
instructions on page 26

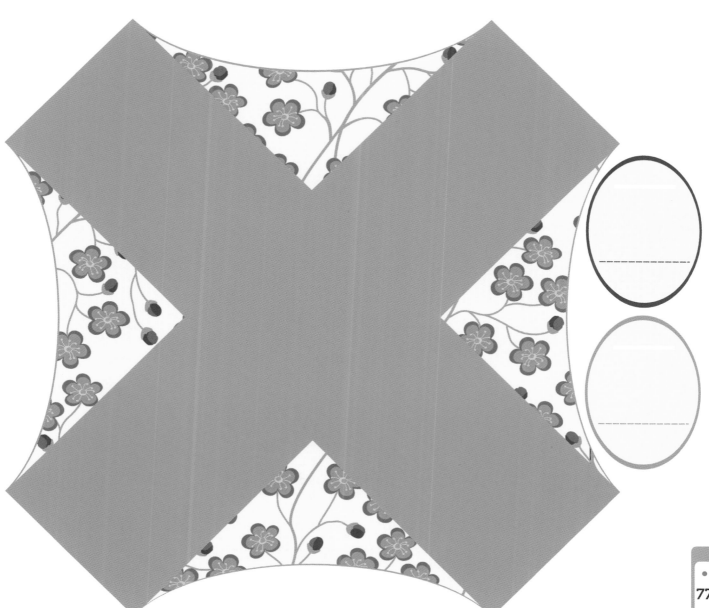

# Surprise (bottom and ribbons)
instructions on pages 30 and 32

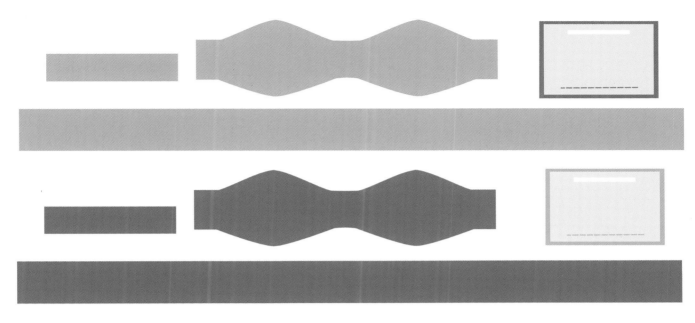

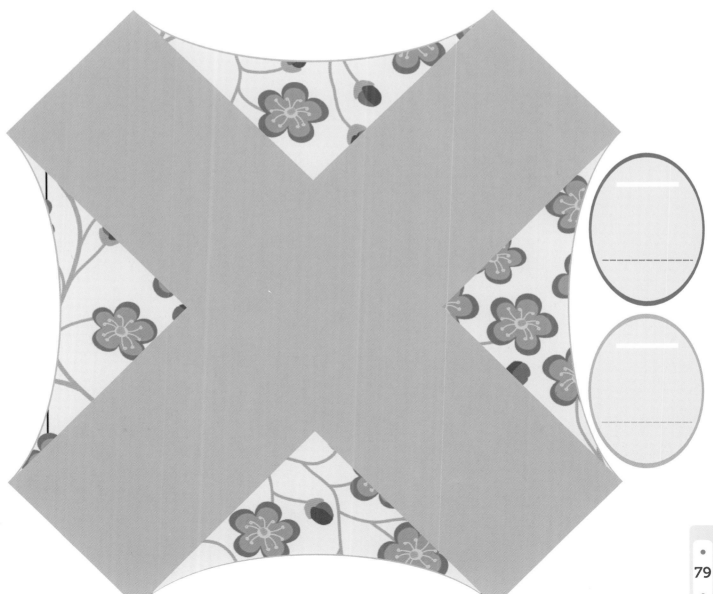